MW01172996

FOREWORD BY
PATRICIA KING

SPEAK
JESUS

THE ONLY NAME THAT CARRIES THE
POWER TO CHANGE THE WORLD

DUSTIN WILLIAMS
HEATHER WILLIAMS

Endorsements

Speak Jesus, by Dustin and Heather Williams, is a book for everyone in this generation. Written from personal experiences, knowledge, and understanding, this book gives insight with biblical clarity that is needed now more than ever.

The chapters are written with readers in mind, recognizing the battles that others have or may be enduring. *Speak Jesus* isn't simply advice given to the readers; it shares scriptural instructions so that readers can activate the Word of God into their lives. I am grateful for the kingdom work Dustin and Heather created in this book.

Speak Jesus isn't just a story of "how to." It's the application that will shift your life into the fulfillment that God has given you through the authority of His Son.

Ryan Johnson

Ryan Johnson Ministries, Speaker, Prophetic Voice, and Author of: *Illegitimacy (The Battle Over Your Identity)*, *How to Contend for Your Miracle (How Supernatural Encounters and Faith Work Together to Bring Answered Prayers)*, and *Racism: The Church and The Nation*
ryanjohnson.us

Dustin and Heather Williams exemplify the essence of genuine pastors. In *Speak Jesus*, you will read personal testimonies demonstrating how inviting Jesus into life's challenges catalyzes transformation for everyone involved. Moreover, this book will inspire you to embrace a life lived with God at the center.

Brandi Belt
Overflow Global Ministries, Healing Evangelist, International Speaker, Author, Leadership Coach

---

The Bible speaks over and again about the importance of names. Names speak of identity, purpose and even destiny. Sometimes names would be changed... and when they were, it had lasting and significant consequences. Jacob, one of the patriarchs of Israel, was born with a name that meant deceiver and usurper. He walked in this identity and manifested this behavior in his life. But after an encounter with God, where he saw and wrestled with God, his name was changed, and he reflected that new destiny in his new name, which shifted his life into eternal purpose.

The world says, "What's in a name?" God says, "I have called you by name and know you." The very God that wrestled with Jacob and transformed his identity manifested Himself in a personhood that bore the name "Yeshua," which means "He saves." This name, the name we call Jesus in the English language, shook the earth to its very foundations and released the destiny of that name which saved the human race.

In this powerful book from Dustin and Heather Williams, you hold in your hands a pathway to destiny and purpose. For in knowing the power of HIS name, you unlock the power of your own identity.

Benjamin Deitrick
Author, Speaker, Founder of Ignite Ministries
International

———————————————

Do you have tests and trials going on in your life, relationships, finances, or career? (Of course you do, we all do at times.) Then you will want to dive into Dustin and Heather Williams' book *Speak Jesus*. Their stories, testimonies, and insights reveal how you can SPEAK JESUS to any challenge you're facing. Dustin and Heather even include crafted prayers at the end of every chapter to help you SPEAK JESUS to key areas and situations. Don't put up with the enemy any longer. And stop trying to deal with it all on your own. Use the power available to you in the Name of your Healer, Deliverer, Provider, and Protector. SPEAK JESUS!

Robert Hotchkin
Author, Speaker, Robert Hotchkin Ministries / Men on the Frontlines
roberthotchkin.com

In my years of knowing Dustin and Heather, I have seen them serve and love the church beautifully. They truly are the fruit of ones who speak Jesus into the hearts and lives of their children, family, friends, and community. The simplicity of this book and message are necessary for the times we are living in. To speak Jesus is to know the power of the One who comes to bring love and victory in every situation! I'm excited for you to dive into this book.

Jamie Lyn Wallnau

Wife, Mother, Author, Speaker, Illustrator &
Podcast Host

We say, "There is power in the name of Jesus," but what does this mean in the day-to-day grind of life? Does it matter how, when, and where we speak the name of Jesus? Dustin and Heather invite you on a journey through *Speak Jesus*. As you read through the pages, you'll find they share their story with a refreshing level of authenticity, vulnerability, honesty, wisdom, and a chuckle mixed in for good measure! You'll find your voice in this wild post-modern world and confidently speak the name of Jesus.

Rev. Ruth Hendrickson
Founder RHM International and Mashah Ministry
Author of *Positioned; How to be Aligned and Empowered to Walk into your Divine Destiny* and *Everyday Prophetic*

Speak Jesus is a living testimony that still decrees of the power of Jesus in their everyday lives. The Williams have so beautifully unpacked what it looks like to allow the name of Jesus to speak triumphantly through their own lives. They make it so applicable to everyone who reads this book with real practical insight that will yield transformative fruit in the lives of believers who apply these principles through faith in the name of Jesus.

Francisco and Deserae Arboleda
Lead Pastors of Shiloh Fellowship

For the last several years, I have had the privilege of walking with Dustin and Heather Williams as dear friends. It is from this perspective that I read their new book *Speak Jesus*.

You will find that it has been crafted from a true shepherd and pastor's heart. It reads like a beautiful devotional blended with relevant Bible study and inspirational stories. It is filled with accounts of personal experiences and is sure to strengthen your faith and faith in the Name (Acts 3:16).

I have often said that God speaks only one language—He speaks "God." This simply means that, as the prophet Isaiah articulated thousands of years ago, God's thoughts are so much higher than our thoughts. His ways are higher than our ways. The apostle Paul declared that now, in the New Covenant, as God's people we have the mind of Christ (1 Corinthians 2:16).

Speak Jesus is a tool that will help you think more like the Lord, and it will help you speak His language, the language of faith. My prayer for you is that as you read this book that your heart will be strengthened with God's grace and filled with His peace that surpasses all understanding.

Derek Ott
Senior Minister at Awaken Apostolic International

———————————————

Dedication

To Our Children, Aiden, Ryder, and Sadie:

We pray that the words within this book serve as a testimony to our faith in Jesus and our love for Him. May this book serve as a reminder that Jesus binds our family together. Just as we call on His name in times of joy, laughter, sorrow, and every other moment in between, as you grow older, may you always know to call on the name of Jesus to find your strength and your peace. Never forget that you are loved beyond measure. Our hope is that the words in this book will inspire you to always keep Jesus first and to always call on His name. We love you more than words, and it is our highest and greatest honor in life to be your parents.

Love,
Mom and Dad

Foreword

I have known Pastors Dustin and Heather Williams for several years now and have worked closely with them for the last few. I know them to be solid, stable, and trustworthy servants of the Lord who walk in humility and faithfulness. They have three wonderful children, and they, as a family, are true models of Christ's nature to their community.

The message of this book, *Speak Jesus,* is so vital in this hour of chaos and confusion. The world is struggling and never has the gospel of Jesus Christ been as needed as it is now. Jesus is the answer to all life's dilemmas, and He is the only way for humankind to be reconciled to their Creator.

Jesus Himself stated emphatically in John 14:6, "I am the way, the truth, and the life and no one comes to the Father except through me" (NIV). Some might say that this is an arrogant statement to be made by a mere human, but Jesus is not a mere human. The apostle Peter in Acts 4:12, boldly proclaimed to the Jewish leaders in his day, "Nor is there salvation in any other, for there is no other name under heaven given among men by which we must be saved" (NKJV).

The apostle Paul confidently declared in Philippians, "That at the name of Jesus every knee should bow, of things in heaven, and things in earth, and things under the earth; and that every tongue should confess that Jesus Christ is Lord, to the glory of God the Father" (2:11, 12 KJV).

Dustin and Heather wrote this book to stir your faith in the simplicity of the power that the name of Jesus has to save, deliver, grant victory, and be all you need to live a full and abundant life. His holy name is worthy to be declared with faith through love and sincere affection for Him and His kingdom.

I fondly remember the night I received Jesus as my personal Savior and Lord. I was in a sad state indeed, feeling bound, oppressed, and completely unworthy. I heard the gospel that night at a Bible study where those in attendance shared how Jesus came into their hearts, forgave them their sin, and gave them a brand-new life within. I so wanted that but wasn't sure if He would want me. I wondered if I had crossed the line of "no return" due to my numerous sins. I humbly asked Him to come into my life and immediately, without any hesitation, He did!

It was as though "liquid love" flooded my heart, and I felt Him remove all my sin and guilt in that instant. I felt so pure, so beautiful within and because of overwhelming gratefulness, I wept all night.

The very next morning, I was busy, "speaking Jesus." I shared Him with my neighbors, friends, and family. No one told me I needed to—it was simply the appropriate response of my heart. He had given me new life. He forgave me for all my sin. In the midst of my hopelessness and helplessness, He gave me a glorious future and a hope. What a wonderful Savior! I continue to speak Jesus every day of my life as He IS my life!

Jesus is the answer for every questioning heart. He is the Light that can penetrate the darkness of this world, but without anyone to "speak Him," the masses will likely never get to know Him. Your voice is needed to boldly speak JESUS! He needs you... the world needs you.

Through this book you will be inspired to embrace all Jesus is and all He does. As a result, I'm confident you will be stirred with passion to tell others. Let's together, "speak Jesus!" He is so worthy!

> *How then shall they call on him in whom they have not believed? and how shall they believe in him whom they have not heard? and **how shall they hear without a preacher?** and how shall they preach, except they be sent?*
>
> —Romans 10:14-15 KJV

—Patricia King
Patricia King Ministries
Author, Speaker, and Mentor

Table of Contents

The Name of Jesus

(DUSTIN WILLIAMS)

Jesus, a name that is known around the world. One name that means so much to billions. Also, a name that makes billions angry, fearful, and frustrated. Still, no matter how He is viewed by you or the world, this name, His name, carries significant weight and power. Jesus was and is the most important person in history. While many try to explain away the stories of the Old Testament as "folk stories," the existence and history of Jesus was recorded beyond even the four eyewitness accounts that account for the Gospels.

My history with Jesus started at a very early age. Both of my parents didn't really have a relationship with Jesus, but both had enough knowledge to know that when you raise your kids, it was always good to throw in a little Jesus-faith and Jesus-religion. So they sent me to a little Assemblies of God church in the small Colorado town of Fruita. They chose that church purely on location, as it was across the street and 200 yards from our door. The added benefit was also having met the pastor, as he and his family lived next door to the church and were pretty active in the neighborhood. The pastor and his family didn't seem too fazed by our poor and rough exteriors or my beer drinking, party animal parents.

As I attended Sunday school at the age of three, I began to learn about Jesus and how He died for me and the sins of everyone. I learned about how He loved me and wanted to live in my heart. I learned that with Him in my heart I could go to heaven. As a 3-year old, that sounded rather odd and at the same time amazing. I thought wow, I can have Jesus in my heart! After all, I watched a lot of He-Man, and I could see how a normal man could turn into an invincible warrior who wore a speedo. I wasn't sure about the speedo, but I was sure I wanted Jesus and the power of eternal life! Over the next few years, I'm sure I asked Jesus into my heart every Sunday. I remember a moment when I was 5 when my heart leaped, which I count as my salvation moment. It was on this day that I took Jesus home, walked up to my dad, who was nursing his second beer of the afternoon, and spoke these words, "Dad, you need Jesus."

When you are a child you don't really understand the power you have to effect change. You don't understand faith; you just have it. Little did I know that at this moment I would plant a seed in some very hard soil. While my dad did not get saved in that moment, something shifted in him when I spoke the name of Jesus. It would change the trajectory of the life he had known up to that point. It's funny to hear him recount that moment this many years later as a fellow pastor. He often reflects on how those words echoed in his head and how the name Jesus revealed an empty part of his heart that needed a real connection with his heavenly Father.

Jesus was foretold by the prophet Isaiah and was prophesied to be Immanuel, which means "God with us." This book is a testimony to the God who has been with me and you from the very beginning. His name has the power to save us from our sins and to break every stronghold. His love truly surpasses all human understanding. He is truly the God who is with us and the God who is for us.

CHAPTER ONE

Speak Jesus: The Power to Save

(DUSTIN WILLIAMS)

I love a good superhero movie. Who doesn't? It's hard not to, especially with the special effects available these days. As much as I enjoyed Adam West as Batman when I was a kid, I much prefer what the studios are putting out nowadays. On top of sweet CGI, Marvel and DC are creating a great universal feel where all our favorite heroes can interact and even save the world together. I enjoyed every single Avengers movie. It's funny though, how many times in those movies the world is on the brink of destruction. From evil CEOs to aliens, the earth is constantly under attack and therefore needing to be saved again and again. Now while these are all fictional movies, they do reflect a certain chord of history we have seen in the real world.

Over the years we have seen civil wars, world wars, nuclear weapons, terrorism, and genocide, which humanity has had to overcome and is still overcoming.

While we may not be facing the threat of Ultron, we are facing a constant darkness that is trying to consume the world as we know it. It is an ever-present threat; the moment sin entered this world there has been a ticking time bomb. Believer and non-believer alike can feel it. While non-believers look for a savior in government and social institutions, believers in Christ look to the promises mapped out for us in the Bible. One of my favorite life verses and reminders is found in the book of Ecclesiastes, which is one of the Old Testament books of wisdom.

He has made everything beautiful in its time. Also He has put eternity in their hearts, except that no one can find out the work that God does from beginning to end.

—Ecclesiastes 3:11 NKJV

I love this verse because it speaks to ALL people having a stake in eternity. We KNOW deep down that there is MORE to our simple being. We are in a fight for the souls of this world and implanted in all of them is knowledge put there by God. When we start sharing Jesus to non-believers, we are speaking to a part of them that instinctively knows that this life is not the end; the answer to eternity is far bigger than our temporary life here on earth. Even as I write these words, our world is facing major challenges that threaten to drag millions and even billions to hell. Whether from personal choice, cultural influence, radical ideology, or the worship of other gods or false religions, billons have never heard the name of Jesus. Does our world need saving? Yes, over and over again.

As a youth pastor in the early 2000s (that feels weird to say), I often referenced Ecclesiastes 3:11 in sermons because I could tangibly see questions about eternity in every student we ministered to. Our youth ministry was full of fatherless students with less-than-ideal home lives and very little offered to them by their parents about the Bible or knowledge of God. Yet the power of the Holy Spirit kept drawing them in, week after week. Every service I would give an invitation to receive Jesus, and students would respond. Why? Because God had already marked them with eternity, and that mark made their response to Jesus possible upon hearing God's word. After all faith comes by hearing, and hearing by the word of the Lord (Romans 10:17).

Some of the places our students came from often shocked me because while I didn't grow up in a perfect home, I did grow up with both a mother and father who loved me, loved God, and did their best to raise us in the church. I remember the first time I met one of our students. Let's call him Dan.

Dan started attending our youth ministry when he was 14 years old. Dan lived with his mom, who was gay, as well as her gay partner and an older sister. They lived in a very small two-bedroom house, and Dan's room was the living room couch. His closet was a suitcase and a backpack. Dan never met his real father but did have a very small relationship with a stepfather from his mom's previous marriage. His stepfather tried to be there for Dan while he was young, but once he started a family with his new wife that all changed.

Dan was exposed to alcohol and drugs from an early age, and he never had a curfew. Most of the time he stayed with friends and often lived briefly in different places. His mom really didn't care in the same way most parents do, though I believe she did love her son. Basically, Dan was in many respects unwanted by so many of his family. Statistically speaking, he would have been given little to no chance at success in both life, family, and in faith simply based on not having a father. When you add the other dysfunctions of the home, his chances became non-existent. But God had a better plan.

When Dan came to us, immediately he was drawn to our family dynamic, and he fit almost immediately. It was remarkable how much he grew as a Christian and as a leader that first year, and it wasn't just because he wanted a family dynamic. It was because he encountered the author of family, Jesus Himself. Shortly after he encountered Jesus, my wife and I committed to giving him rides home (20 miles round trip) and making sure that he could attend camps, retreats, and events, even if that meant for our family to sacrifice financially. We were committed to see this young man grow into everything God was calling him to be.

This is what Jesus is capable of: taking a young kid that doesn't have a chance in the world's eyes and bringing new life and destiny to them. Nobody had to chase him down; he just had a couple of Jesus-loving friends that invited him to church, and the rest is history. Often we can get so overwhelmed as believers when it comes to bringing the good news to the world. After all, we know the challenges and we are aware of the need. But that is the beautiful thing about Jesus. He invites us to be fishers of men, and fishing doesn't take a microphone, stage, or videos with awesome lighting. It simply takes a person to cast a line into a sea of desperate souls. We don't change the world by packing stadiums full of people; we change it by sharing Jesus with those around us. While this seems small, if every believer in the world won just 3-4 people to the Lord in a year, the world would be saved in one year... THE WHOLE WORLD!

Now as Jesus was walking by the Sea of Galilee, He saw two brothers, Simon, who was called Peter, and his brother Andrew, casting a net into the sea; for they were fishermen. And He said to them, "Follow Me, and I will make you fishers of people." Immediately they left their nets and followed Him.

—Matthew 4:18-20 NASB

As a pastor, my primary responsibility is to help shepherd the flock. Yes, I preach/teach messages... yes, I counsel people... yes, I take care of various departments. While this is a great honor and privilege, I am still sharing Jesus because I am first and foremost a Christian. Just the other day, my wife and I had one of our son's friends lose a very expensive Apple watch at our community pool. Not only did he forget to grab it after swimming, but it took him a full 48 hours to realize he had lost it. Luckily, his parents pinged it before it died, and we had an area of houses where we thought someone might have found it and taken it home. So, my wife and I prayed and asked God for help, after which we went to knock on the first door. A lady by the name of Danelle answered, and we explained our story. She replied, "We found it and hoped someone would ping it. After all we are God-fearing people in this house." We answered, "Us too, and we pastor at a local church!" Long story short, her family had not been attending church for the last 2 years and now we are there at her house inviting her to attend... God literally pinged her house for our meeting. Not only that, but our son's friend and his family got to see the power of prayer in action.

There is an important verse that should define all believers and Christians:

> *Preach the word! Be ready in season and out of season. Convince, rebuke, exhort, with all longsuffering and teaching.*
>
> —2 Timothy 4:2 NKJV

This verse has very little to do with a titled position and everything to do with added expectation. We are called to be ready to preach the Bible and encourage others in a moment's notice. This is true not only on good days but bad days as well.

One of my favorite athletes is Tim Tebow. As a native Coloradan, I naturally cheer for the Denver Broncos and was excited for them to draft Tebow. Tebow is not a talented QB, but he's an amazing hard worker. His first season as the starter in Denver was one filled with dramatic finishes. The Broncos would be getting creamed for 3 straight quarters of play, after which became what the fans coined as "TEBOW TIME." He would often lead comebacks and help push the Broncos to a win. At the end of the day, hard work beats talent when talent fails.

This is also true when being a witness for Jesus. How you pray and study His word in the secret place will help you cultivate a Jesus lifestyle. Every successful pastor and leader I know didn't start out with a mic in their hand but rather willing hands to do whatever it takes for people to know Jesus. That might be helping a single mom move or pushing a broom and setting up chairs at your church. It might be volunteering to help at your local food bank or public school. Whatever door the Lord opens, you can be ready. When we position ourselves like this, we can decree, "IT'S JESUS TIME."

LET'S PRAY

Jesus, I thank you that You are the light of the world. It's Your light that I want to shine through me. When You say go and where You say go, may I be quick to listen and obey so that people can come to know You as their Savior. Here I am Lord, send me. I choose to follow You all the days of my life! In Jesus' name, amen.

FOR FURTHER STUDY:

1. Praying for the nations—Psalm 33:12

2. Praying for leaders—1 Timothy 2:1-2

3. Praying for the church—Acts 2:42

4. Praying for ministry workers—Acts 6:3-4

CHAPTER TWO

Speak Jesus Over Fear

(HEATHER WILLIAMS)

I remember it like it was yesterday—my first panic attack. I was 12 years old and I had just recently been reunited with my father. He decided to take me on a trip to visit my aunt whom he hadn't seen in years. I was so excited for this trip. It was going to be the exciting father/daughter trip I had always wanted to have. The trip turned out to be exciting all right, but not in the way I was hoping or expecting.

We had driven all day and finally arrived at my aunt's house. I went to my room and as I was lying on the bed, I began to feel sensations I had never experienced before. My heart was pounding out of my chest, my breathing became rapid, and my mind was racing as a million thoughts went through my head. I began to get hot and sweaty, and I was just sure that my heart was going to pop out of my chest. In the midst of all of these sensations, I began to feel scared, unsure of everything around me. I wanted to leave the room, but I was terrified to leave it. I later learned that sensation was my "fight or flight" response kicking in. I stayed in that room for what felt like hours, but I'm sure it was only a matter of minutes.

There were a few more times after that during the trip when I felt like I couldn't breathe, but it never made any sense to me. Being the age of 12, I guess I just thought everyone, at some point or another, isn't able to catch their breath. I didn't say anything to my dad or my aunt, but I would go on to have three more panic attacks on that trip alone. Thankfully, when I returned home after the trip, everything went back to normal, and I didn't say a word to anyone about what I had experienced.

The summer I was 18, I went on another trip. This time I traveled with friends from my youth group to Pensacola, Florida for a youth conference. One particular day, we went to the beach to hang out and have some down time when suddenly I had a strange, yet familiar feeling. I knew I had experienced it before, but I couldn't quite remember it. My chest felt heavy; I felt like I couldn't breathe again. My friend told me, "Your lips are blue!" That was all I needed to hear to really go into panic mode. Again, it felt like forever before I could calm down, but I finally did.

When I returned home, I told my mom about my experiences with these strange sensations on both occasions. She scheduled me an appointment to see our family doctor, and after many tests, I was officially diagnosed with panic attacks. It was at this moment the doctor handed me a script and said, "Try this. It'll help kick your brain back into order." My 18-year-old brain wasn't sure what I had been handed, but when I saw the word *Prozac* I understood. He had prescribed a small dose of an antidepressant to help me get through the attacks.

I left my doctor's office, went to the pharmacy, filled the prescription, went home, and took my first pill. The moment I swallowed that first pill I knew that it would be my first and my last. I wasn't going to take any more. It wasn't that I had issues with antidepressants, or that I felt they were wrong for a Christian to take (more on that later), but I wanted to figure out what was going on in my own brain and spiritual life that could be causing these issues. I was determined to do it all on my own.

The following months I deeply researched panic and anxiety attacks: the causes of them, what triggers them, and what could make them go away. I tried everything I could—no caffeine, hot baths every night, herbs, vigorous exercise, and the list goes on. In those days, when my heart rate would elevate due to the exercise, it would bring on a panic attack. The pounding in my chest from the exercise felt like a panic attack, so, the next thing I knew I'd be in a major panic attack, all from trying to fix my panic attacks. The irony! Nothing I did worked, but I can say that after about 10 months, my panic attacks went away. How or why, I still don't know.

Sadly, at the age of 23, the panic attacks again returned with a vengeance. This time they became debilitating. With every panic attack, I thought I was either dying or going crazy. I could not get a full breath, my hands tingled, fear immediately set in. I was convinced I was having a heart attack because my heart was racing.

Defying rational thought, I became someone that my parents and husband had never seen. Then, I became pregnant with my firstborn, Aiden, at the age of 27. Pregnancy in and of itself can make any woman crazy, right? But this time I got hit with absolutely brutal panic attacks. We found out later that issues with my hormones were causing hormone-induced anxiety while pregnant.

I remember one day when Dustin was leaving for work and I had Aiden and now my second child, Ryder, home with me. I was just certain that if he left for work, I would die, and the kids would be alone and in danger. It was one of my worst panic attacks to date. I was sobbing, couldn't think straight, and was a hot mess. I told him, "I'm going to have to go to work with you. Because if I die, I'd rather you be close, so the kids have an adult around instead of a tragedy happening at home." It was irrational thinking on all levels, but it was my perceived reality in the moment.

There were seasons in my struggle with these attacks that I wasn't able to go to the store alone, sit in church, or even be left home alone at times. If you're reading this and wondering how in the world a person can get to this level of fear, I don't blame you. If you've never dealt with panic or anxiety attacks, I pray you never do. If you have dealt with them or if you are currently dealing with them, let me just encourage you right here and now; there is hope, there is freedom, and there is healing!

Because of my history of panic attacks, seeing people set free from fear and panic has become a huge passion of mine. You might be wondering if I ever got freedom from panic attacks, and the answer is YES!

In 2018, I went to a retreat for women in ministry. I was so afraid of having a panic attack in an airplane that I drove 11 hours to get to the retreat instead of flying the two hours.

At the end of the retreat, they asked if anyone wanted prayer. I requested prayer for my panic attacks. They prayed for me and that was that. Someone had a word for me; they saw God taking a power washer to my mind. There wasn't any lightning strikes or loud thunder from heaven, but I did know in that moment that God had answered the longing of my heart to be set free. I went home and told my husband I had been set free.

The real test would be a couple weeks later when our family would be flying to Hawaii. Due to my panic attacks, I had never been able to fly. I'd stress about the flight days in advance, and it was a miserable experience for my husband to fly with me. But this trip was different. When we landed in Hawaii, my husband looked at me and said, "Who are you and what have you done with my wife? You haven't panicked one time on this trip."

He was right! I hadn't panicked once, and it was awesome! I had a newfound freedom. A freedom I had longed for, prayed for, and received prayer for so many times before. God had answered my prayers.

That was in 2018. In all transparency, there have been several times since that the enemy has tried to convince me I've not been healed. Rick Warren has said to turn your mess into a message, and this is what I've done by writing about my struggles with panic and anxiety. Even when the devil comes at me with fear and panic, I remind myself (and the devil, for that matter) that I have victory because who the Son sets free is free indeed!

If you're reading this and struggling with fear, let me just say you are not alone. God has not forgotten you. His plans for you are good, and His plan for you is freedom. That freedom can only be found in and through Him. He died on the cross for your freedom and for your salvation.

I remember the day that I realized I could either be a person of fear or a person of faith. You can't operate in both at the same time. The devil may try his hardest to get me to operate in fear, but I choose to be a person of faith. And you can choose to be a person of faith too! No matter how deep the struggle with fear, no matter how far gone you may feel you are, with Jesus' help, you too can overcome fear!

LET'S PRAY

Jesus, I come to you and surrender my fear to you. You know I've struggled with it, and I choose to give it to you. I repent for the times I have partnered with fear instead of faith. I choose to be a person of faith and not of fear. When I'm tempted to surrender to fear, may your peace and your presence surround me and pull me out. I give You my every desire and need to control and choose to trust in You and Your good plans for me. In Jesus' name, amen.

FOR FURTHER STUDY:

1. Fear is not from God. —2 Timothy 1:7

2. Jesus does not leave me alone when I am afraid. —Psalm 23:4

3. Jesus delivers me of my fear. —Psalm 34:4-8

4. God alone is my refuge and strength. —Psalm 46: 1-3

5. I can trust in Jesus when I am tempted to be afraid. —Psalm 56:3-4

CHAPTER THREE

Speak Jesus in Mercy

(DUSTIN WILLIAMS)

Have you ever been intentionally wronged? This might seem like a dumb question because I think it's safe to say that everyone has. Now when these wrongs are accidental, we can usually deal with that. Why? Because we have all unintentionally hurt people around us. Because we ourselves need mercy in these moments, it is easier for us to extend it to others. However, when horrible things are done to us intentionally and with malice it hits different. Maybe you are like me, and you also have a strong righteousness gene. Maybe you are more like Mr. Rodgers, who never had any conflict in his neighborhood. Either way, I am working to be more like Jesus when it comes to mercy.

I understand that we all need mercy. In and of itself, the cross Jesus died on is a symbol of mercy. It was the death that we all deserved because of our own wicked sin nature. Jesus didn't just die for the "kinda bad," normal people like many of us consider ourselves to be. He died for the worst of the worst, the best of the best, and everyone in-between. He extended mercy to those who will never receive it. He gave to all without strings attached. All the while, He knew that we would need continual mercy even after accepting Him as Lord and Savior. That is how broken we are because of sin: in order for us to walk with Jesus, we need our daily dose of mercy.

One of the things God has taught me about mercy is that mercy is not just a pathway to forgiveness, it's also a powerful gift that God gives us to break strongholds. Not just for us personally, but for the world around us.

One of the best examples of this is found in Luke 18:35-42 (NIV) as a blind beggar calls out to Jesus.

As Jesus approached Jericho, a blind man was sitting by the roadside begging. When he heard the crowd going by, he asked what was happening. They told him, "Jesus of Nazareth is passing by." He called out, "Jesus, Son of David, have mercy on me!" Those who led the way rebuked him and told him to be quiet, but he shouted all the more, "Son of David, have mercy on me!" Jesus stopped and ordered the man to be brought to him. When he came near, Jesus asked him, "What do you want me to do for you?"

"Lord, I want to see," he replied. Jesus said to him, "Receive your sight; your faith has healed you." Immediately he received his sight and followed Jesus, praising God. When all the people saw it, they also praised God.

We see here a man who cries out, "Mercy," to get the attention of Jesus. He was desperate to see; he was done stumbling around and begging for a living. He needed something to change. What is the most amazing part of this passage? Jesus didn't lay hands on the man. He didn't make a mud spitball like in another miracle. He simply came into agreement with mercy. The mercy of God is far greater than just forgiveness of sins. It is the power to heal!

I grew up with a popular saying, "Lord, have mercy!" It was used to describe high stress problems in our house. I can even hear the voice of the Tyler Perry character Madea saying in my head, "Lort, have murcy." While there is nothing wrong with using this plea with everyday stresses, we cannot ignore its power when contending for healing. LORD, HAVE MERCY is and can be a powerful decree for a breakthrough. Several years ago, my mother had a shoulder injury that severely handicapped her ability to do the simplest of things. My wife and I had just had the first of what would be mom's three grandkids, and she was determined to hold those babies. It was in this moment that God gave her a mercy strategy! She began covering her shoulder in prayers of grace and mercy throughout the day whenever she felt the pain. Slowly but surely her shoulder was healed without surgery or therapy. Not that those things are bad, but Mom felt that mercy for her miracle was her assignment. God had already showed her the healing; mercy was the catalyst for the breakthrough!

We all need to get better at receiving mercy and declaring it over sickness and pain. The Bible tells us that mercy triumphs over judgment (James 2:13). This is key in understanding that we don't have to judge our sickness and pain, and chalk it up to old age or an "oh well, that's life" mentality. So many times, we accept the judgment of living in a sin-cursed world because we are just going to deal with sickness and pain. While this is true in the natural, it is not a true judgment in the supernatural. If you are struggling physically, I want you to simply pause and declare mercy over the pain right now.

MERCY GROWS MATURITY

As a father, I have begun to understand that when mercy is extended, it increases signs of maturity. I've noticed that when I show my children mercy instead of judgement, they often are quicker to turn from whatever disobedience they have committed. This doesn't mean that we don't discipline them, but it does mean we walk them through consequences that fit their crimes. When we have opportunities in life to extend mercy, it causes us to gain a godly discipline that we all need to have. When people sin against us, owe us, or hurt us, we can choose a higher level of love and forgiveness.

A few years ago, I received a speeding ticket, but I wasn't speeding. The police officer wasn't even doing speed checks when he pulled me over for going 15 miles per hour over the speed limit. I assured the officer that I wasn't, in fact, speeding. I had just turned onto the street and hadn't even gotten up to the speed limit yet. (I am still convinced he just mixed me up with another vehicle.) In the end, the officer gave me a ticket and told me I could take it up with the judge. That is exactly what

I planned on doing, so I marked my calendar and waited for my day of justice.

Unfortunately, I marked the wrong date for court and showed up a day late. To my dismay, I now had a warrant out for my arrest, which isn't the best look for a pastor. I set up an appointment for the next day and knew that not only was I going to get in trouble for missing court, but there was also no way the judge would believe I wasn't speeding; after all, only criminals miss court dates! (I'm kidding.) Having no idea how warrants for traffic tickets work, I was preparing myself for jail and considering some tattoos to help me fit in.

I remember standing before the judge and pleading my case on not only missing court, but how I wasn't speeding. To my surprise, the judge sided with me and dismissed the ticket. The judge did, however, fine me for missing court, which was far less than the price of a ticket.

The judgement I was expecting was far different than what I received. The judge was kind and caring. He was even-keeled and had compassion. Not just for me but for others who went before me.

I was immediately reminded of Matthew 18:

Therefore, the Kingdom of Heaven can be compared to a king who decided to bring his accounts up to date with servants who had borrowed money from him. In the process, one of his debtors was brought in who owed him millions of dollars. He couldn't pay, so his master ordered that he be sold—along with his wife, his children, and everything he owned—to pay the debt. But the man fell down before his master and begged him, "Please, be patient with me, and I will pay it all." Then his master was filled with pity for him, and he released him and forgave his debt.

—Matthew 18:23-27 NLT

As I was shown mercy that day, I also have a responsibility to have mercy for the officer that stopped me. That's why I concluded that he must have confused my car with someone else's. When we don't show the same mercy that Jesus has given us, we are like the servant who begged for forgiveness and mercy but never learned to give it in return. We see that later in Matthew 18 when that same servant was unable to extend the same kind of mercy to a fellow servant. Once the king caught word of this, he removed the mercy that had been extended.

Shouldn't you have mercy on your fellow servant, just as I had mercy on you? Then the angry king sent the man to prison to be tortured until he had paid his entire debt. That's what my heavenly Father will do to you if you refuse to forgive your brothers and sisters from your heart.

—Matthew 18:33-35 NLT

LET'S PRAY

Father, you remind us that mercy triumphs over judgment (James 2:13b). I decree that same mercy over every part of my being. Justice was paid for me through the blood of Jesus, so I call down that same mercy. In Jesus' name, amen!

THE KEY TO GROWING IN MERCY

God blesses those who are merciful, for they will be shown mercy.

—Matthew 5:7 NLT

Jesus gives us a very simple key to growing in mercy: just be merciful. Easy to say, much harder to do. When was the last time that the car that intentionally cut you off got a merciful pardon by you and not a silent (or not-so silent) "idiot" out of your heart?

As I write these words, I am speaking to myself as much as I am to the readers of this book! You see, mercy is easy to give when the person that causes the offense wants forgiveness; it's much harder to give to someone undeserving. Yet that is what Jesus did on the cross. He gave mercy to all of humanity even though not everyone would accept it.

If we are to be like Jesus, we too must be willing to extend mercy in the same way, knowing that those around us don't deserve it and knowing that they may never accept it. This is why mercy must become a posture of the heart. As we wrap up this chapter, let's ponder how we can speak mercy into a world that desperately needs to see and experience *true* mercy.

LET'S PRAY

God, I come to you asking for mercy. I know I need Your mercy every day, and I'm grateful that Your mercy never runs out. Your mercies are new every morning. Help me to be quick to extend mercy and to show mercy to others. May I be a carrier of Your mercy everywhere that I go. In Jesus' name, amen.

FOR FURTHER STUDY:

1. Mercy for the nations —Matthew 9:13

2. Mercy for leaders —2 Corinthians 12:9

3. Mercy for the church —2 Corinthians 13:14

4. Mercy for the sick —Luke 18:35-42

5. Mercy for the lost —Titus 3:5

CHAPTER FOUR

Speak Jesus in Forgiveness

(DUSTIN WILLIAMS)

One of the most powerful statements in all the Bible is, "Father, forgive them, for they know not what they do." In this moment, Jesus could be talking specifically about those who have just put Him on the cross, but we can rightly assume that this statement served a greater purpose and was for humanity in general. What is interesting in this statement is that Jesus is talking directly to His Father.

A little later, we see Jesus calling out, "My God, My God, why have You forsaken Me." This marks a change in relationship during the hour when the sky turned dark, and silence covered the ground. As the Son of God, Jesus interceded on our behalf through a cry of forgiveness. God's response to that prayer was to remove His favor from Jesus, so that He could bear all the sins of the world. The Father could not look at Jesus, because to look at Him was to see every dirty, little, secret sin of humanity.

It really is a beautiful display of the love Jesus has for us, "While we were still sinners, Christ died for us" (Romans 5:8 NIV). We deserved the darkness, the rejection from the Father, but Jesus took it instead. Even as I write these words, it's easy to tear up just thinking about what Jesus did for me so that I could be a son reunited to his heavenly Father. It is through His great forgiveness and mercy that we are also challenged to do the same. Forgiveness is not a suggestion in the kingdom of God—it's a requirement. There are two main areas that I believe are some of our biggest struggles in this area.

FORGIVENESS OF SELF

Personally, I have always struggled with forgiving myself, and I believe many people who have chosen blatant sin in their past do the same. While I grew up in the church, I began to live a double life as a young man around the time I turned 17. I went to church on Sunday (out of obligation to my parents) and lived for the world the other 6 days a week. I had a good job, money, and friends, and we were all about the next party. I chased alcohol, girls, and fast cars, all while punching my Sunday attendance card at the end of each week, often hungover. During this season of my life, I was so angry at the church, I was angry at religion, and I was tired of trying to be what my pastors and parents wanted me to be. I began to seek family and connection amongst those I partied with and eventually joined a car club that was more of a front for a local gang. I was living much of this lifestyle (somewhat) secret to my parents and completely secret to people at church.

One night, it all changed. I had hit a new low. I looked at my life and realized that my current life trajectory looked very bleak. What I had been doing didn't matter in this world. I had a Solomon moment, and suddenly, everything seemed pointless. I no longer wanted what I had experienced in this world. It left me empty. It was in this moment that I had a face-to-face encounter with the love of God. In an instant, God's love and forgiveness entered me, and I was delivered of everything. I prayed a simple prayer, "God, whatever is left of me, you can have it all." God then reminded me of the call on my life. Soon after my encounter, our youth pastor at my home church came up to me and asked if I had ever been called to preach.

In that moment, I knew that God was following through on my commitment to Him. This began an invitation to start an internship at my church. I am forever grateful that God used this pastor and church family to help re-establish my call to preach the gospel. However, while I had received God's forgiveness and love, I had not fully forgiven myself. I was terrified of running into people I had partied with, people I had hurt, and even people I had threatened. I was afraid that old friends wouldn't understand. I was afraid that I had gone too far, and because of my past choices I could never be all that God was calling me to be. I thought about all the people I hurt, lied to, and cheated on. God had forgiven me, but I had not forgiven myself.

This affected me in ministry and even in my marriage for several years until my wife, who knew of my past, encouraged me to reach out to a few of my old party buddies and past relationships. I was terrified but decided to listen to her advice. As I began to send messages and letters, hoping people still had their old numbers, I literally felt a weight lift off me. I didn't reach everyone, but I got ahold of the ones that mattered. I was blown away at the love and forgiveness I was shown by some of my old friends and girlfriends. In an instant, my ministry changed and grew, my marriage got better, and I began to let go of the past and the embarrassment I had carried.

FORGIVENESS OF OTHERS

As a Christian, this seems like a no brainer. After all, Jesus literally tells us in Luke 6, "Do not judge, and you will not be judged. Do not condemn, and you will not be condemned. <u>Forgive, and you will be forgiven</u>" (v. 37, CSB).

Those final words, "Forgive, and you will be forgiven," are placed just after Jesus tells those around Him not to judge or be condemning. Our view of righteousness is often reflected in our own personal view of fairness. What we view as fair is often centered around our flesh or what I like to call the "me factor." Jesus was constantly teaching us to value others over ourselves, and while I agree, it is not always how I feel. That is why we mustn't judge situations based on feelings alone. Feelings can be hurt, and feelings can also carry memory. The word of God is very clear on forgiveness—it's non-negotiable. We are to offer it even when the other party is 100% wrong. I want to give you a few examples that make it hard for believers to forgive because they're justifiable.

EXAMPLE 1: CHURCH HURT

Church hurt is a very real issue in modern-day ministry. Many people have walked away from relationships, ministries, and leaders for a myriad of reasons. I am certainly not saying people need to stay in toxic church environments, but sometimes we can't forgive someone for hurting us when they claim to follow the same Jesus that we do. Church hurt doesn't just happen to church goers or volunteers; it happens to ministers, too.

As a minister, I have had some very vile and hurtful things said both to my face and behind my back. Both church goers and fellow leaders have hurt me. I have also wanted to walk away from ministry all together because of how people have hurt me. In the natural, it would have been justified, but because I know that I have been called to preach the gospel, I can't allow the words of a few broken people to damage God's call on my life. If I know who I am according to the Father and I know what I am called to do, then I must also walk in this truth:

forgiveness is not earned, it is given. If Jesus can freely give His life for all of broken humanity, I can certainly forgive a few rude, broken, and hurting people that didn't know what they were doing or saying.

EXAMPLE 2: OFFENSIVE ATTACKS

What about those who constantly attack believers and intentionally hurt others? I have many extended family members who honestly believe our family is brainwashed. We don't drink, we don't curse, and we keep talking about our faith. This has created a rift that has uninvited us to certain family functions. Not one time have we attempted to push our own convictions on them; my family just didn't partake in what bonded the rest of them as a family. I went years without seeing grandparents and cousins because we were "crazy Christians."

As a former youth pastor, I often watched students suffer in public schools for their faith. I see it now with my own teenagers at home. Being a Christian is not popular on Instagram or TikTok these days; if you voice your faith online, you are often ridiculed. The Bible tells us to forgive, and we will be forgiven (Matthew 6:14-15), and to bless those that persecute us (Romans 12:14).

Forgiveness isn't acceptance of the past; it is living as Jesus did that day on the cross. When Jesus died, He wasn't just giving His life for the sins of the world at the time. He was shedding His blood for the sins of today and tomorrow. He died for horrible sins, sins that I probably can't even imagine, even the sin of persecuting and mocking Him.

Politically, the church is slowly being targeted as the "root" of all problems in modern-day wokeness. I see a very frustrated church in the United States, one that is trying to fight against culture and demonic policies. While I can easily feel this way, the Lord has been challenging me to pray for the forgiveness of our nation. It isn't a surprise to God that the church is being targeted; in fact, He sort of wrote it all out for us in the Gospels. Forgiveness is what we are called to, even amidst all the shaking and growing darkness, and that is exactly what we must do.

LET'S PRAY

Jesus, I repent of unforgiveness. Forgive me for the times I have withheld forgiveness because of hurt or offense. God, would You help me to be quick to forgive. Even though I've been hurt, I thank You that because of the cross and Your deep love, I can forgive. I choose to forgive today. In Jesus' name, amen.

FOR FURTHER STUDY:

1. We forgive those who have hurt us. —Matthew 9:13

2. We forgive those who have persecuted us. —2 Corinthians 12:9

3. We forgive ourselves. — 2 Corinthians 13:14

4. Mercy for the sick —Luke 18:35-42

5. Mercy for the lost —Titus 3:5

CHAPTER FIVE

Speak Jesus for Mental Health

(HEATHER WILLIAMS)

Growing up, mental health wasn't a subject that was preached on. I truly can say that I don't recall hearing a sermon on the subject until recent years. Because the church hasn't talked about it, people are left feeling isolated and alone and, more times than not, suffering in silence.

Thankfully, in recent years, I have seen this subject talked about more in the church. I remember the day that I preached a message on mental health, and the response was unlike anything I had ever experienced. Countless people came up to me, thanking me for my vulnerability and for sharing my story.

So many had felt so much shame and condemnation as they had struggled in silence in the church, feeling too guilty to talk about their struggles. Please trust me when I say that I know this is a hard subject to talk about. It is so hard to air what feels like dirty laundry for all to see and hear and, since you're holding this book, even to let someone read. But I can say this, and I can say it with confidence: one thing I have learned, especially as a parent, is that if we as the church (and as Christians) don't talk about the hard stuff, the world will, and they will be the one writing the narratives on these hard topics. The church needs to be the ones writing these narratives, not the world.

I didn't have much experience dealing with mental and emotional pain outside of panic attacks until after the birth of my third child. Although panic attacks had been a battle for me, I never really understood other mental struggles. That spring, I found myself sitting with my doctor in his office explaining to him a strange set of emotions and uncharacteristic feelings that were new to me. I knew something was off, but I wasn't prepared for his answer. I thought he'd tell me he was going to run some bloodwork because I was low on vitamins or something of that nature. What he said next shocked me. "Well Heather, you are in a moderate depression and a state of burn out."

I just looked at him and said, "Me? Depressed? No way. I'm not the depressed type. And burnout? What does that mean? I'm just tired. Of course, I'm tired. I have three young kids, so who wouldn't be tired?" He went on to tell me that all my symptoms pointed to his diagnosis and that I needed to take a break from my current position to allow my body to rest and heal. (Just a side note, he did look at some recent bloodwork to rule out what I was thinking was the issue.)

I left his office that day doing the only thing I knew to do besides pray, and that was research. I was going to learn all that I could on depression, burnout, and everything in between. I learned that depression is a mental battle and if left untreated can become a debilitating mental illness.

To better understand this subject of mental illness, let's first define what mental illness is. A mental illness can be defined as a health condition that changes a person's thinking, feelings, or behavior (or all three) and that causes the person distress and difficulty in functioning.

Before I learned about mental illness, I had the preconceived idea that if one had a mental illness, it would be obvious. That's actually not the case at all.

People can look just fine on the outside, but on the inside, they feel like they are trapped in a nightmare.

A common misunderstanding about mental illness is many people think it's rare. However, the surgeon general reports that mental illness is so prevalent that in fact very few families in the U.S. are not affected or untouched by it in some way.

- According to recent estimates, approximately 20 percent of Americans, or about one in five people over the age of 18, suffer from a diagnosable mental disorder in a given year.

- About 3 percent of the population have more than one mental illness at a time.

- About 5 percent of adults are affected so seriously by mental illness that it interferes with their ability to function in society. These severe and persistent mental illnesses include schizophrenia, bipolar disorder, other severe forms of depression, panic disorder, and obsessive-compulsive disorder.

- Approximately 20 percent of doctor's appointments are related to anxiety disorders such as panic attacks.

- Eight million people have depression each year.

- An estimated two-thirds of all young people with mental health problems are not receiving the help they need.

Clearly mental health is an issue that needs to be addressed, but I firmly believe it needs to be addressed by the church. In writing this chapter, it is my deep hope and strong desire that we can look at mental health from a biblical perspective. You'll never see in the Bible the exact words "mental health." But what you will find is many people in the Bible struggled with some very intense emotions that were more than just a passing mood. David and Job specifically come to mind. David in the Psalms wrote about some very intense feelings.

Here are three things to remember about mental illness and what to do if you or someone you know is going through a mental health crisis.

1. MENTAL ILLNESS IS A RESULT OF SIN BUT IS NOT ITSELF A SIN.

We live in a fallen world. Adam and Eve caused us all to be born into a life of sin. Because of sin, we have all the terrible issues that we face today. I've heard people blame God for all these issues, but the reality is that we live in fallen world, and we are a people born into sin. Because of sin, our bodies don't always work correctly.

2 Corinthians 4:16 says, "So we do not lose heart. Though our outer self is wasting away, our inner self is being renewed day by day" (ESV). Our outer self is wasting away. That means at times our bodies absolutely fail us and leave us with frustrations and questions, needing help.

Our body, although created by God in incredible detail, is not going to live forever. Our brain is part of our body and, at times, can fail us. I won't go into all the scientific explanations and descriptions about the brain and mental health. Please do research it if you'd like— it's incredibly interesting. In short, there are countless neurons and synapses firing in the brain at any given time. Just like a heart can give out or a pancreas stops making insulin, the brain is just as susceptible to having its own set of issues as well.

It's a natural, human characteristic that when people are suffering, other people want to help. I can't even begin to tell you some of the crazy things I've heard people say, all in an effort to help, but it actually didn't help. Let me give you an example. If someone I was talking to had a headache, I wouldn't tell them that it was a result of sin in their life. If someone has diabetes, I wouldn't tell them that it's the fault of sin in their life.

In the same respect, just because someone is suffering with a mental illness, it doesn't mean they are struggling because they are living a life of sin. I remember I was told at one point that I had unconfessed sin in my life because I was battling panic attacks at the time. I can assure you that I didn't have any unconfessed sin in my life. We can go ahead and add that to the list of what NOT to tell people who are struggling with a mental health issue (or any health issue, for that matter).

2. GOD HAS NOT LEFT, ABANDONED, OR REJECTED THOSE WHO SUFFER WITH A MENTAL ILLNESS.

It's very easy when you're going through a struggle of any kind, to think that God has left you. In fact, one of the devil's greatest tactics is to get us to believe that God has left us. What I can for sure tell you, because I've lived through it, is that God has not, and He will not, ever leave you or forsake you.

It is the Lord who goes before you. He will be with you; he will not leave you or forsake you. Do not fear or be dismayed.

—Deuteronomy 31:8 ESV

Can a woman forget her nursing child, that she should have no compassion on the son of her womb? Even these may forget, yet I will not forget you.

—Isaiah 49:15 ESV

You have searched me, Lord, and you know me. You know when I sit and when I rise; you perceive my thoughts from afar. You discern my going out and my lying down; you are familiar with all my ways. Before a word is on my tongue you, Lord, know it completely. You hem me in behind and before, and you lay your hand upon me.

Such knowledge is too wonderful for me, too lofty for me to attain. Where can I go from your Spirit? Where can I flee from your presence? If I go up to the heavens, you are there; if I make my bed in the depths, you are there. If I rise on the wings of the dawn, if I settle on the far side of the sea, even there your hand will guide me, your right hand will hold me fast.

—Psalm 139:1-10 NIV

Nothing in that chapter or anywhere in the Bible indicates that God leaves us in the hard times. In fact, it's just the opposite.

Psalm 34:18 says, "The Lord is close to the brokenhearted and saves those who are crushed in spirit" (NIV). Because God has not forsaken or left those struggling with a mental health disorder, the church, the body of Christ, shouldn't forsake or leave them either. At times that may look messy. At times, there may be people who come to your church and make it their home. Those people need to have a safe place and need a place to belong.

3. GOD'S PLAN FOR MENTAL ILLNESS IS VICTORY.

Although I don't know why not everyone with health issues or mental health issues gets healed, I do know God desires us to live from a place of victory. I can also say that God's plan for the believer regarding *any* issue is victory. This doesn't apply to just mental health.

Anything that has been done to us in the past or what we've gone through or will go through holds little power compared to what was done for us on the cross.

But he was pierced for our transgressions, he was crushed for our iniquities; the punishment that brought us peace was on him, and by his wounds we are healed.

—Isaiah 53:5 NIV

I used to repeat this verse all of the time when I was going through my panic attacks. Even though it doesn't say, "by his wounds we are healed *in our mind*," it surely means it. By His wounds we are healed, in any area that we may need healing in.

Jesus' death on the cross is a finished work. What that means is there's nothing we can do to add to our salvation. We don't have to work super hard at anything to gain a bigger or better life in Christ or in eternity. He handled our victory; He *is* our victory and because of His death and resurrection we can have victory in every area of our life.

WHAT TO DO IF YOU OR SOMEONE YOU KNOW IS STRUGGLING WITH MENTAL HEALTH...

1. Get in God's presence every day.

You do this by reading His Word every day, by praying every day. Even when you don't feel like it. Especially when you don't feel like it.

> *Do not conform to the pattern of this world, but be transformed by the renewing of your mind.*
>
> —Romans 12:2 NIV

You renew your mind by reading His Word. I can't even begin to tell you what a lifeline the Word of God is. Especially in the dark and trying times.

Often when we are facing a battle, the Bible is the last resort and can be the one thing that gets neglected. But the Word of God is living and active, which means it can speak to you right where you are. You can read the same verse time and time again, and each time it can do something new for you because God's Word is alive and just as powerful today as the day it was written!

2. Don't isolate.

Isolation is the enemy's plan for you, not God's! For years I isolated myself when I was going through my panic attacks. In fact, I rarely talked about it unless I was very, very close with someone.

One day in my prayer time, I felt like God spoke to me and told me that isolation is one of the enemy's greatest tactics. When you're isolated, you lose your sense of community, hope, belonging, identity, and so much more. If the enemy can isolate you, he can wreak all sorts of havoc on you and your mind, so commit to yourself that you won't isolate yourself.

If you're helping someone going through a mental health crisis, don't let them isolate themselves. Show up in their lives, be consistent and present, even if you think it isn't helping or it doesn't matter. If you are the one struggling with mental health issues, please do not stop going to church or engaging with the people and the community around you that loves you so very much.

Sometimes we think we have to be perfect. Especially as Christians, it can be easy to fall into the trap of having to look or act perfect. Social media has made this even more of an issue. But sometimes we need to remind ourselves that what we usually see on Facebook or Instagram are highlight reels, not real life.

It's ok to not be ok and really, there's no better place to not be ok than in church. If we all had to be perfect to go to church, every church building in the world would be empty on Sunday mornings because no one is perfect.

3. Get help.

If you are struggling with a mental illness, please know you can get help. In fact, please do get help. I know how hard it is to seek and ask for help. A great place to start is your primary doctor; see what they recommend. If they recommend medicine, that's for you and God to decide if that's the course you need to take. If you do get on medicine, please don't tell yourself you have a lack of faith or need to get closer to Jesus or that God is disappointed in you. If someone needs medicine for migraines or pain, there's no shame in that, and there shouldn't be shame in medicine needed for mental health.

A counselor is another great way to receive help. There was a period in my life where I also received biblical counseling. Having a trusted professional that you can process with can be a great part of breaking through into your healing.

Jesus wants you to have victory in your mind. We can have victory and victory is ours for the taking! Jesus Himself is our victory. And even on the days when the struggle is real, Jesus has not left you and He never will!

LET'S PRAY OVER MENTAL HEALTH

Jesus, Your death on the cross secured the victory that I can have in my mind. You are my victory, and today I choose to stand on that victory. Jesus, I repent of believing the enemy's lies that I can never be free. Forgive me for thinking You've left me or abandoned me. Your Word says I have the mind of Christ. Today, I choose to live that out. In Your name, I pray, amen.

FOR FURTHER STUDY

1. I have the mind of Christ. —1 Corinthians 2:16

2. Jesus is my peace. —John 16:33

3. I am a new creation in Christ. —2 Corinthians 5:17

4. Jesus shows me mercy and grace in my time of need. —Psalm 103:8

5. God's Word guides me in all areas of living. —Psalm 119:105

CHAPTER SIX

Speak Jesus with Holy Spirit

(DUSTIN WILLIAMS)

Jesus didn't just come to die for the sins of the world. He came to be the forerunner to Holy Spirit moving in and through us. His blood was the catalyst for us to be able to harbor the very presence of God. When we walk in the fullness of the Holy Spirit, we are carrying the authority and testimony of Jesus Himself.

I once had my friend, Jayme Montera, break it down to me like this: "So many times we wear our Christian t-shirts, our cross neckless, and our scripture tattoos... let's just remember, we are not called to 'wear' Jesus. He desires to wear 'us.' So much so that the world doesn't just see you, they see Him." When we are allowing the Holy Spirit to dwell in us, we look more and more like

Jesus. I have seen this firsthand in many saints that have pioneered the gospel.

Growing up, I would hear about and listen to amazing preachers like Oral Roberts, Billy Graham, and Reinhard Bonnke. However, where I saw the greatest example of Jesus was in my grandma Champlin. She was an amazing tongue-talking, holy-rolling Pentecostal. She loved without strings attached, and when I walked away from my faith, she prayed me back. In fact, she prayed many prodigals back into relationship with Jesus. She knew the power of not only the name of Jesus but the Holy Spirit that carried His authority.

Jesus didn't die and rise three days later so that we could have a good story to celebrate. He died for the sins of all mankind so that they could be filled with the living Holy Spirit of God. For this reason, we are not fighting against the world, we are fighting for it. The enemy doesn't care how "saved" you are; he is coming for your soul and the lives of the people you love regardless.

Some believe that the Holy Spirit and the power of the Holy Spirit in the book of Acts were only for the first-century church. I just don't and can't see it that way. I have experienced and witnessed far too much with the Holy Spirit. I have seen addictions gone in seconds never to return. I have seen sickness healed. I have seen salvation happen to the hardest of hearts. All the while declaring the name of Jesus in power.

But you will receive power when the Holy Spirit has come upon you; and you shall be My witnesses both in Jerusalem and in all Judea, and Samaria, and as far as the remotest part of the earth.

—Acts 1:8 NASB

The primary reason Jesus came was to testify to the love and nature of God. He did this through the healing of the sick, through the casting out of demons, and through feeding both body and spirit. The disciples were some of the first to witness this, and we are witnessing it today through His Word. This is the reason the name of Jesus carries power and authority—because it testifies over the accusations of hell and the grave. His blood truly speaks a better word, and His Spirit knows no limit.

MY TESTIMONY OF THE HOLY SPIRIT

Reinhard Bonnke once said, "Humans were not meant to depend on human strength alone... When God created us He did it with intentionality of us being power assisted." To me this is what it looks like to live with the Holy Spirit dwelling on the inside of us.

My first car was a 1977 Toyota Celica, and not the cool-looking Celicas we know today. This car went 0 to 60 in about 4 minutes. It didn't have power steering; it was all made of steel and weighed about 10,000 pounds, which meant I couldn't do U-turns very well and parking was sometimes a challenge.

Imagine my surprise when I upgraded vehicles and discovered the world of power steering. I went from steering with my own strength to steering with the power of assistance through "POWER STEERING." The power of the Holy Spirit similarly transforms our lives when He upgrades us.

Jesus said that you shall receive "power" to be my witnesses. That means we allow the Holy Spirit to help guide and direct our steps, and when we do, the testimony of Jesus goes out. Holy Spirit power is the upgrade we all need to boldly speak the name of Jesus. My testimony is not just of salvation, but of radical transformation that can only be attributed to the supernatural. When people hear and see the power of God, they are introduced to who God really is. This is why we speak about Jesus.

There is power in the name of Jesus and, when proclaimed, it has the power to bring freedom from sin, heal the sick, and raise the dead.

When I was 11 years old, we had an evangelist by the name of Brother Watson visit our church. This was the first time I had seen a visible demonstration of the power of the Holy Spirit. As the altars filled with hungry people, I witnessed people falling down, speaking in tongues, and getting set free from demonic strongholds. I witnessed those who walked with canes and walkers healed. I wasn't familiar with the Holy Spirit, but I knew at the young age of 11 that I wanted it!

I went down front to receive the baptism of the Holy Spirit and was immediately struck down by the tangible presence of God. I laid there on the floor for what felt like hours, praying in the Holy Spirit and speaking in tongues. For the next 4 weeks, Brother Watson stayed with us and every night our church came together for revival meetings. Our church was transformed by this move of the Holy Spirit and, though it was already a large church, it seemed to double in size. Our church was on fire for God, and that fire lasted several years.

While many were marked and changed for the better, everyone didn't stay that way. Revival has a way of cleansing and humbling you, and it also has a way of bringing people closer together and building strong friendships. These are all great things, but don't forget the enemy of our souls is always looking for footholds into our lives.

Sometimes when a move of God happens, and you witness and walk in power of the Holy Spirit, you can be susceptible to a little thing called pride. You see, our church had an amazing choir, and during our revival that choir went to a new level. They were already well known, but their popularity grew even beyond our region.

As presence turned to pride, we began to see sin enter in, and a handful of strong believers fell into sexual temptation. It started as rumors of affairs at first and then boiled over into our young adults and youth ministry. It was a terrible season in our church where awful sin was running wild. When the leadership tried to deal with it, they were blamed for the problem. All our pastors either were forced to resign or were fired. Families got divorced, youth rebelled, and I walked away from church.

As I witnessed this, I became bitter over the Holy Spirit move that I had experienced. While it was very real to me, I felt like the push for signs, wonders, and miracles had somehow created the problem. So many men and women of God that I looked up to had let me down, and so many of my friends in our youth group had fallen into sin. After a while, many of the teenagers in our youth ministry were engaging in sexual sin. How could a church that had experienced such a move of God for so many years fall so hard? Where was God in all of this?

> *But if you do not do so, then take note, you have*
> *sinned against the Lord; and be sure your sin will*
> *find you out.*
>
> —Numbers 32:23 NKJV

This is exactly what happened to us in our church. So many were "found out," including in our youth ministry. The problem wasn't limited to our youth ministry, but it was blamed for much of it. In fact, everyone pointed to one person, and while she was guilty of sin, she was hardly the only one. When she (only she) was asked to apologize in front of the whole church for her part in the sexual sin that involved several young people and at least 2 adult leaders, I was extremely angry. She had already repented to leadership, but she was now the fall girl for the church. All the while some choir members, who had divorced their spouses and had affairs, still sang in the choir and taught Sunday school, unaware pastors were blamed and fired, and many others had developed a reputation for drinking and partied excessively. Where was the justice in this? Why were some exposed and others not? After all, who is God that He should be mocked?

Needless to say, this is where I walked away from the church and the things of the Holy Spirit, which I referenced in an earlier chapter. Now you might be reading this and think, *I don't blame the kid.* In my own self justice, I can agree with you, but self-justification is a pitfall to pride. The very thing I was angry at had entered me, and it stole from me years of walking with the Lord. It stole from me my foundation and tried to forfeit my calling. It calloused my heart to Holy Spirit to the point that I wanted nothing to do with Him for years, even after I returned to God and my church family. But God in His mercy is so good!

God restored my call, brought me my wife Heather, and healed my heart from church pain. To make a long story short, God not only restored me, but He helped restore my home church. Today I am so thankful for every pastor, leader, and teacher that poured into me. That church that was torn apart is today one of the largest churches in the area with several community outreaches, not to mention a youth ministry that is on fire for God and has even become famous on TikTok for making "Holy Spirit Activate" into a viral trend.

RE-ENCOUNTERING THE HOLY SPIRIT

Years later as I was serving as a youth pastor, I took a group of teenagers 400 miles away to a youth convention in Colorado. I had been in my share of camps and conventions and was prepared for our teens to get away and encounter God. Little did I know that this particular trip was going to re-introduce me to the power of the Holy Spirit.

As the altar call was given, some of our youth and leaders responded by going to the front while I stayed in the back with the others. I began seeing people fall and weep, things I had been used to seeing years before. Then one of our leaders (Marcie) led the evangelist over to our youth group. I thought, *Ok, this might be awkward.* The evangelist came up to me and said, "Marcie asked me to come pray with you, but I have a word for you first."

To be honest, I immediately put my guard up. I didn't even realize it, but I was still closed off to the gifts of the Holy Spirit. As he began to prophesy over me, every hard area began to fall, and I felt the Holy Spirit moving like never before. When he finished, he had us join hands with our teens, and we prayed for fresh fire to fall on us. That's when a Holy Spirit grenade went off, and each of us were thrown on our backs. It was an experience that I will never forget and that has stuck with me for the last 18 years. That was the day I was re-introduced to the power of Holy Spirit, and it marked and changed our youth ministry.

After we returned, we experienced revival and transformation in our youth ministry to the point of teens getting filled with the Holy Spirit in our bathrooms and at school. God seemed to lead the most broken and outcast to us, and we got to introduce them to Jesus and an encounter with Holy Spirit.

POWER ASSISTED

Can you be saved and not be filled with the Holy Spirit and still call on the name of Jesus? Yes, you most certainly can, but why miss out on the very power Jesus rose to give you? Jesus ascended into heaven so that the

Holy Spirit would come and live in all of us, and it really is the only way I know how to do this "Christian" thing. When I call on Jesus, I am expecting an answer because the Holy Spirit is my connection. That connection gives me boldness to speak Jesus wherever I go and in whatever circumstance I walk through.

LET'S PRAY

Holy Spirit, our Living Hope, we long for Your glory and power. Our hearts long to be overcome by Your presence. Like a mighty rushing wind, fill me and baptize me with Your fire. Spirit of Truth, teach me all things and bring to remembrance the Words of Jesus. In Jesus' name, amen.

FOR FURTHER STUDY:

1. We allow the Holy Spirit to search our hearts. —1 Corinthians 2:10-16

2. We ask the Holy Spirit to guide us. —Romans 8:14

3. We submit ourselves to the Holy Spirit's will. — Galatians 5:18

4. We speak boldly by the Holy Spirit. —John 16:13

CHAPTER SEVEN

Speak Jesus: His Name Is a Powerful Weapon

(DUSTIN WILLIAMS)

I was once told by my lead pastor that as far as spiritual battles are concerned that you are either in one, coming out of one, or getting ready to step into one. Not only have I found this to be true, but I also notice it in my own life. So regardless of how you feel about spiritual warfare, it is happening now. This is why we are given this command in Ephesians:

A final word: Be strong in the Lord and in his mighty power. Put on all of God's armor so that you will be able to stand firm against all strategies of the devil. For we are not fighting against flesh-and-blood enemies, but against evil rulers and authorities of the unseen world, against mighty

*powers in this dark world, and against evil spirits
in the heavenly places.*

—Ephesians 6:10-12 NLT

I often start with verse 11 when preaching messages on the armor of God, but let's take a minute and recognize verse 10. "Be strong in the Lord and in his mighty power." I grew up singing songs like "What a Mighty God We Serve" and the "Lord Is Strong and Mighty" or even "Mighty To Save." As a believer, I have learned about all the impossibilities made possible when it comes to the power of God.

Believe it or not, scripture only gives us glimpses of this. We are given enough, however, to understand the unrivaled power the Lord possesses, but we must encounter it for ourselves. Isaiah gives us a glimpse into this when referring to the seven spirits of God (Isaiah 11:2), one of those spirits being "strength" or depending on the translation the spirit of "might." We can safely say that being "mighty" is not just something God can do but it is a part of who He is.

When we call on the name of Jesus, we are literally calling to the very source of might and strength. For this reason, when battles come, we can speak the name of

Jesus with boldness. In fact, we are instructed to call on the name of our Lord to renew our own strength. For years my mom has used this to crush fear in her own life, especially when my dad is driving. When she is startled or scared, she often shouts, "JESUS HELP ME" as a reaction. As a family, we often laugh at her reaction. But this is exactly how we should approach things that come against us!

One of the most powerful scenes from the movie *Braveheart* is when William Wallis, the leader of the Scottish army, is about to be beheaded for leading the charge for an independent Scotland. As the blade comes down, he yells "FREEEEDOM." This is how we should face adversity when it comes to the name of Jesus. JESUS!!

A few years ago, my wife and I were getting ready to take a small ministry trip to Kansas City. My wife had an uneasy feeling about it, but I insisted it was probably the pizza from the night before. As we merged on the I-10, we were forced to go faster than the posted speed as rush hour traffic was rushing. I eventually made my way over to the far-left carpool lane so that I could get out of the craziness and drive the speed limit.

That is when we heard a loud noise and the driver's side front of my truck dipped into the road. In a flash, my entire wheel had come off, and I began to pray. It was as if the world slowed down; I was fully aware of the heavy traffic on my right and fully aware that my wheel and tire were now rolling beside me. As I began merging into the median, I had a vision of my wheel and tire (which had picked up speed) hopping over onto oncoming traffic and smashing through the windshield of a small silver car, killing the person driving.

What happened next was supernatural to say the least. The very fact that time slowed down and I was fully aware of every side of my car, including the traffic alone, still gives me chills. Inside of the awareness I had full control and was safely pulling over without hitting other vehicles—this was a miracle in and of itself—but it was the words coming out of my mouth that had seemed to carry a greater authority. I decreed Jesus and, in my heavenly tongue, commanded the missile of a wheel and tire to stop. The wheel itself had cleared a small barrier and was on a collision course with oncoming traffic, until it hit what I can only describe as an invisible wall. The wheel came to a rest in the middle of the median, and we were able to safely pull over.

What happened in 30 seconds seemed like 30 minutes. The prayers that came out of my mouth surpassed anything that I could have prayed in the natural. Every word, both in English and in tongues, carried a supernatural authority. I went to war that day in the spirit, and the Holy Spirit answered. I had no other option; I needed to fight for my family and those on the road and I believe I witnessed the spirit of might (see Isaiah 11:2).

To this day, I weep when I think about how that tire hit an invisible wall and how God was so good to every other driver near me. After all, God's promise to Joshua and Israel is the same today:

One man of you shall chase a thousand, for the Lord your God is He who fights for you, as He promised you.

—Joshua 23:10 NKJV

When crying out the name of Jesus becomes natural, we are actually partnering with the supernatural nature of God. Jesus is more than a name, or a story; He is God Himself and through His death and resurrection, we can carry victory with us wherever we go. The Bible tells us that whatever flows out of the heart a person speaks; I want to be so consumed with Jesus that when tragedy strikes, this is what comes out. When I smash my thumb with a hammer, my flesh may want to curse but my heart needs to be the one who speaks.

As you may know, there is an amazing song called "I Speak Jesus" by a worship collective group out of Nashville. While this book was written apart from this song, it drives the heart of this book home so well.

Dustin Smith (great name by the way), who helped produce the song, said in an article by Integrity Music said, "As writers, we can have a tendency to overcomplicate everything. It is good to do our best when writing songs to describe Jesus in the most awesome and majestic ways possible. But at the end of the day, the words all fail to compare to His greatness. Sometimes the best thing we can do is say His name and be captured again by the wonder of who He is. Just speaking the name of Jesus over our families, our communities, and our situations are some of the most effective things we can do."

"The song came as easy as it sounds," shares Smith. "Jesse Reeves prayed over us before we started writing and just said, 'I just want to speak the name of Jesus over these people.' That was it. The whole prayer. Nothing more. Nothing less."[1]

Below are the main lyrics to *I Speak Jesus* by Here Be Lions.

I just want to speak the name of Jesus
Over every heart and every mind
'Cause I know there is peace within Your presence
I speak Jesus

I just want to speak the name of Jesus
'Til every dark addiction starts to break
Declaring there is hope and there is freedom
I speak Jesus

'Cause Your Name is power
Your Name is healing
Your Name is life
Break every stronghold
Shine through the shadows
Burn like a fire

---

[1] "Here Be Lions Releases Sophomore Project – I Speak Jesus EP – Available Now." 2019. Integrity Music. September 23, 2019. https://www.integritymusic.com/news/2019/9/23/here-be-lions-releases-sophomore-project-i-speak-jesus-ep-available-now.

I just want to speak the Name of Jesus
Over fear and all anxiety
To every soul held captive by depression
I speak Jesus

Your Name is power
Your Name is healing
Your Name is life
Break every stronghold
Shine through the shadows
Burn like the fire

Shout Jesus from the mountains
Jesus in the street
Jesus in the darkness over every enemy
Jesus for my family
I speak the Holy Name
'Jesus'[2]

These are powerful decrees to sing and speak to the power of His name. As believers, we know that because

---

[2] *I Speak Jesus* by Here Be Lions written by Jesse Reeves, Dustin Smith, Abby Benton, Carlene Prince, and Raina Pratt. *I Speak Jesus* lyrics © Integrity's Praise! Music, All Essential Music, For Me And My House Songs, September 2019.

of Jesus, we have the full authority to speak in His name according to His will.

I write these things to you who believe in the name of the Son of God so that you may know that you have eternal life. This is the confidence we have in approaching God: that if we ask anything according to his will, he hears us.

—1 John 5:13-14 NIV

God's will is that none should perish and for all to have everlasting life. In addition, God's will is for His people to be blessed and highly favored. God's will is for you to live and walk in full victory and confidence for every battle that comes your way.

LET'S PRAY

Heavenly Father, come and open my eyes so that I might see how great You are and how complete Your provision is for this new day. In the name of Jesus, I take my place with Christ in the heavenlies, with all principalities and powers (powers of darkness and wicked spirits) under my feet. Because of You, I have the victory and I walk in victory. In Jesus' name, amen.

FOR FURTHER STUDY:

1. We decree victory in every battle. —James 1:12

2. We submit our outcomes for His outcome. —Romans 12:19

3. We commit to the battle. —Deuteronomy 20:4

4. We speak Jesus over every circumstance. —John 16:33

Acknowledgments

We'd like to express our deepest gratitude to all of our family and friends who have enriched our lives so that only eternity will fully tell the depths of their impact. Their unwavering love, support, wisdom, and advice have shaped us into the people that we are today.

To our incredible parents, who instilled in us the values of faith, love, and perseverance. Your guidance and love have been the foundation upon which this work stands. Thank you for leading by example. We love you!

To Pastors Jim and Carrie, your wisdom, leadership, and mentorship over the years have impacted us deeply. Thank you for never giving up on us.

To Patricia King, the love you carry for people and for Jesus has caused us to want to love better. Thank you for allowing us to be part of your life and for loving us so well.

To Ruth Hendrickson, your godly insights and perspectives have enriched our lives to the fullest. Thank you for always giving your time so freely, even when it has been inconvenient. Thank you for always cheering us on, not letting us give up, and for always pointing us to Jesus.

About the Authors

Dustin and Heather Williams are both ordained ministers and have been in ministry for over 20 years. They have pastored in Colorado, Utah, and Arizona in various roles ministering to children, youth, young adults, and families. They have a heart to see people come to know Jesus as their Savior and to walk in the fullness of who God has called them to be so they can influence their everyday world.

Dustin is passionate about preaching and teaching the Word in very practical ways. Heather loves to mentor and teach and is an incredible team builder. Together they complement each other, both in ability and calling.

Dustin and Heather live in Maricopa, Arizona with their three beautiful kids, Aiden, Ryder, and Sadie. They currently serve at Shiloh Fellowship Church as Executive Pastors.

To connect with Dustin and Heather, visit speakhope.org.

Pay It Forward

W e're absolutely thrilled that you took the time to read our book. We pray that it brought you hope and gave you a strategy to overcome obstacles in your life.

Now, we have a humble request that would mean the world to us. Would you please take a moment to help others discover the transformative power of *Speak Jesus* by writing a review?

Your words, straight from the heart, hold immense value. Your contribution can make a significant impact on the lives of those who come across the book.

Thank you for being part of the journey to share these kingdom principles with others.

Go to: www.amazon.com/review/create-review.

Made in the USA
Columbia, SC
16 February 2025

53912756R00059